In the opening poem here the poet is on a train journey, the world outside seems "all snow," and in the darkening train-window he sees his own face "after midnight, haggard and vague,/ reflected against anonymous woods." As the final two lines in a book's first poem these are hardly typical, they're neither elegant nor elegiac, but what they are is *exact*, and the reading of them just filled up my trust-space, they moved straight into that space saying *this is worth doing, this is where today starts mattering, you can stay inside lines like these and for a while all will be well.*

There's also a very moving father-and-son poem called "Breathing and Reading," the first line of which is "The father has read the son many books." Full-stop, you'll notice. A writer only starts and stops this bluntly when he's thinking inside one of his deepest secrets. The poem names some of the books this father and his small son have been sharing and goes on with, "Now in silence the son turns pages/ fingertips pressing the edges of a story," continues with "so son and father, pillow-propped, cradle/ different books, shoulders and legs touching," and rises into, "The father knows nights will come/ when the son wants to tumble into sleep alone/ so he doesn't budge."

Anything more you need to be told about the quality of *The Watchmaker's Table?* I don't think so.

— Don Coles

Other books by Brian Bartlett

Poetry

Travels of the Watch (2004)
Wanting the Day: Selected Poems (2003)
The Afterlife of Trees (2002)
Granite Erratics (1997)
Underwater Carpentry (1993)
Planet Harbor (1989)
Cattail Week (1981)

Books Edited

Earthly Pages: The Poetry of Don Domanski (2007)
Don McKay: Essays on His Works (2006)

BRIAN BARTLETT

The Watchmaker's Table

Edited by Anne Compton.
Cover illustration copyright © Andrea Gingerich, istock.
Cover and interior design by Julie Scriver.
Printed in Canada on 100% PCW paper.
10 9 8 7 6 5 4 3 2 1

Library and Archives Canada Cataloguing in Publication

Bartlett, Brian, 1953-
The watchmaker's table / by Brian Bartlett.

ISBN 978-0-86492-508-4

I. Title.

PS8553.A773W38 2008   C811'.54   C2007-906995-9

Goose Lane Editions acknowledges the financial support of the Canada Council for the Arts, the Government of Canada through the Book Publishing Industry Development Program (BPIDP), and the New Brunswick Department of Wellness, Culture and Sport for its publishing activities.

Goose Lane Editions
Suite 330, 500 Beaverbrook Court
Fredericton, New Brunswick
CANADA E3B 5X4
www.gooselane.com

For Ralph and Rita Dahl,
true-blue true-north true-hearts

Contents

The Sideways 8

Given Words

Breathing and Reading

Time, Flying

I'm stuck with the infinity thing
again this morning: a skinny
inexpressible syrup, finer than light,
everywhere present:
— A.R. Ammons, "Syrup"

Instead of hovering forever above, I'd like to feel a weight grow
in me to end the infinity and tie me to the earth. I'd like, at
each step, each gust of wind, to be able to say "now" . . . to have
a fever, and blackened fingers from the newspaper, to be excited
not only by the mind but at last, by a meal, by the line of a
neck, by an ear. . . . At last to guess, instead of always knowing.
To be able to say "ah" and "oh" and "hey" instead of always
"yea" and "amen."
— Damiell, an angel,
in Wim Wenders' film *Wings of Desire*

The Sideways 8

All the Train Trips

All the train trips I made in those years, alone,
   along one province-to-province, through-the-night
      route: the swaying, the braking, the shunting,

snacks in the knapsack, beers in the bar car
   where strangers gathered like survivors —
      houses burned down, families lost. In no time

some called each other "Friend," "Pal,"
   "Funny bastard." The coach seats never went
      back far enough for me to sleep, so after

the hobnobbers' car closed at the border
   and we were rumbling through another country
      I read while midnight faded like some town

sped through, unnoticed in the murk and blur.
   I'll always read Lorca's poems in the light
      of one winter night when the world outside

was all snow — and overlap Aksakov's memoirs
   with one summer night when heat and body heat grew
      until the coach was a kitchen with three dozen stoves.

I've forgotten the names of villages and towns
   I knew only as crows know nests they fly over
      on their way somewhere else. *Black's Point*,

maybe, or *Hackmatack Corner,*
  Moose Junction. Some day will I recall nothing
    but how far in the dark I was? —

sleeplessness, the broken breath of strangers,
  my face after midnight, haggard and vague,
    reflected against anonymous woods.

Night has parachuted you here, onto the seawall.
    You stumble,
regain your footing, your bare feet blue. You spread
    sleep-numbed fingers
through diaphanous air. This was once a place of welcoming
    and farewell,
like any doorstep. Breaking the mist, then slipping away
    just as fast,
ships take possession of a moment again, lit by nothing
    but memory:

    Aquitania   Arosa Star   Athenia   Atlantic
    Baltrover   Bayano   Beaverbrae   Calgaric
    Canberra   Carinthia   Cristoforo Columbo

Watching the fast-forward drift, you think, *Unreal —
    alphabetical!*
A minesweeper made over for refugees, moonlight
    pouring into
the hollow cheeks of the exhausted ones on deck;
    a once-white liner
now a troop carrier, humbled, turned reptile-green;
    a hospital ship
whose wounded are hidden, like flaws inside an egg.
    Up a gangplank
a doctor walks forever, his pale trenchcoat spotted.

Inside the shelter, ticket-takers, guides, and tourists
    have vanished

for the night. Fuzzy light infiltrates, the ceiling distant
    as sky.
Slowly, with whispers and mumbles, with a face flicking
    here, dissolving
there, with a kerchiefed head, a kimono, a battered cap,
    it's all at once
the flush of summer, the burn of fall, winter's nip,
    spring's rush.
Iridescent pigeons of four decades fuss and flutter
    in the rafters,
and the smells of coffee from as many years mix in
    the past-saturated
air, while languages jostle like so many bones clicking
    and clacking
in a shaken bag. You duck to avoid a badminton bird
    knocked back and forth
by two girls in floral dresses and polished shoes, satin
    ribbons in their hair —
as if the crossing were a day trip across a lake,
    the water waveless —
while a boy lying on the floor turns a gas mask into
    a plaything:
goggles with an anteater's black snout.

Your footsteps mute, you think, *Nobody sees me,*
    because I'm alive.
On benches in rows, they wait, wait, biting their nails,
    twisting their buttons.
From drawstring cloth bags — the continent's first gifts —
    soap, razor blades,
toothbrushes, cigarettes, stamps, pencils, airmail forms,
    slip into laps.

Many who don't know Corn Flakes and English
    mistake the treat
for package filler, and spill the flakes — so sounds of
    underfoot crunching
mix with the blessèd rubber-stamp *thump, thump*
    on precious papers.

Beyond the high windows, more ships slide past, your mouth
    shaping their names:

> *Doric   Drottningholm   Duchess of Atholl*
> *Hellig Olav   Homeland   Homeric   Irpinia*
> *Ivernia   Marine Shark   Montcalm   Montclare*

A mascot filly, sporting the banner 8th CANADIAN HUSSARS,
    shakes straw
from her mane, her horseshoes knocking on boards,
    while a war bride
hugs a one-armed man, one-eyed man with a two-part face —
    white, purple.
In the luggage cage, among boxes, crates, and suitcases
    with torn labels
and rusted buckles, a bushy-mustached newcomer paces:
    Brune — ma valise, over
and over, *Ma valise est brune!* A stranger with missing papers —
    Russian, you guess —
shuffles away, a purgatorial furrow in his forehead.
    High above the crowd,
through windows, faces of those barred from entry
    peer in, open-mouthed
but unheard —

Saturnia   Saxonia   Seven Seas   Tanafjord
Thuringia   Transylvania   Tuscania
Walnut   Waterman   Westphalia   Zion

Like an eavesdropping angel, you hear unspoken
    phrases, instantly
translated. A nursing mother touches the fine hairs
    on her infant's scalp:
Romano, dear Romano, born on the Roma!
    From a schoolboy
who wept over leaving the moon back home,
    steady snoring floats.
He sleeps, collapsed against his father: *Ah, son,*
    like we promised,
we tied the moon to the ship. On a bench that can't hold
    one more body
a hunched young woman hearing her name called
    goes pale and
closes her eyes: *Back home that might mean. . . .*
    A bench away,
a grandfather holds an octopus wrapped in a towel,
    unfresh, lovingly brought
from Naples: *A treat for tonight, or tomorrow!*

Face by face, the timeless light restores them all
    while your spectral fingers
touch your spectral face, and you whisper to anybody
    who might listen,
"Hello. I am the only ghost here."

An Offer of Warmth

I'm lying on the couch reading Heraclitus when you start
babbling in the chimney. After breakfast, a fire heated
up the flue, but flames and glow gave way to ash,
warmed bricks saving you from 30-below wind chill.
Your voice amplified, you sound a foot above the grate
though you're likely roosting just inside the chimney top.

Your squeaky, bubbling chatter — unlikely dolphin,
pet-store parrot, look-at-'er whistle, hyped jay.
I just learned Pythagorus recalled his former lives
as cucumber and sardine, so I'm wondering if Heraclitus
might come back as a starling singing in January,
Air dies giving birth to fire, fire dies giving birth
to air. Your concert goes neatly with his quip,
Homer I deem worthy of good cudgeling.

Migration has its glories, but I'm fond of you birds — you fists
of packed feathers — who hang around, weathering out the winter.
Any day you're welcome to whatever warmth I can offer,
especially if down the chimney you chortle, *Mindfulness,*
mindfulness! in your fluent, fractured ways.

6364 Edinburgh St.

Our house, cuboid
   of roundnesses — apple,
clock, thumb-piano

                          Half-moon
                             of peach, staining a page
                             of geometry homework

Four phones in the house
   yet when ringing starts
we run, search, shout

Season of blackouts —
   flashlights in a row:
mother, father, daughter, son

                         Ancestral photos —
                            spider's strand linking
                         grandparents to grandparents

On my son's mobbed desk
   green rubber T-Rex,
fallen on its side

                         Bright light saved them
                            from basement fears. Now
                         they want the dark, with candles

Goodbye, goodbye
    to the old piano —
all its 88 stained keys

                              Rows of books hidden
                                  behind rows of books —
                              secret life of the house

On the Philosophy shelf
    an owl's feather,
great talons curved

                              So tempting to pull —
                                  the chain suspended
                              from the Brazilian monk's bell

How did the King
   lost from the chess set
end up in the compost bin?

                                        Past midnight, I wander
                                          from floor to floor, searching
                                        for a lost cloth sheep

Out of its case,
   propped on its stand, the guitar
stays more in tune these days

Three Candles and a Fan

for Karen, on her 42nd birthday

Three matches lit one by one in the night
The first to see all your face
The second to see your eyes
The last to see your mouth
          — Jacques Prévert, "Paris At Night"

The long heat of August bathes our bedroom
as it bathes the maple and the sycamore.
Candle flames — one for each side table,
the other at the foot — waver in the air
stirred by our faithfully humming fan
that brings relief like water in a drought.
Tonight, abed, apocalyptic thoughts:
I'd want to be, if the heat never dipped again —
if this north became a south —
the last to see your mouth.

Turn your mouth to me in this light
more than half darkness, give me the shadowed
secrets from your neck to your feet.
Oscillating, tracing a reliable arc,
the fan builds up its own breath, a rising
wave on which we ride.
That sound becomes a soothing hum,
an O that tells me now is the minute
to follow our most eager cries,
the second to see your eyes.

Why do I want our three leaping flames
to interrupt the intimate dark —
to see your eyes, more themselves
than windows to anything finer,
eyes that don't choose that seagreen vase
or that book, but my eyes, to trace.
In minutes like these, with the fan's breeze
no match for your fingers and lips,
I could believe I've been laved with grace,
the first to see all your face.

May that cooling machine give us words
new enough for our love: three blades
blurring into a phaseless circle,
generator of moving air, its sea sound
like the source — or the pooling — of all
our sounds, nothing like white
noise, but the gathering of all our
whispers and laughter, and those scritches
awaking our bodies as long as we have sight —
three matches lit one by one in the night.

Walking Laura Home from Daycare

A quarter moon excites her as much as a full moon.
In my arms, she points to a fingernail of light
through the trees. "The clouds," she says,
"are melting into the moon."

From behind, a raw voice stops me cold,
makes me stoop: a crow swoops so low it puffs
air against my neck. It flaps to a hurricane-
split, uprooted tree, then rises skyward
again, rasping. Other days, we've mimicked crows
to hear who makes the most convincing caw
yet that brief outburst at my back left us
speechless. Twice I've had nightmares
in which she was kidnapped, panic and weeping
overtaking me, everyone I talked to disbelieving
and nonchalant. When she says in my ear, "Hungry,"
I recall crows filching unwrapped candies
from the grass, after a Canada Day street party.
In a sunhat and blue dress, she rested in the shade
beside the shattered maple-leaf piñata.

She wants to be held, then struggles, kicks.
When I let her go, she cries, "Run, run!"
I take up her challenge, race heavy-booted, lift
her for a kiss. Last night I read about a boy
whose father called him Rāhula, "Fetter,"
then left him a few days after his birth

to start down tortuous paths to enlightenment.
Rāhula, misnamed child, now it's you I'd talk to,
not your father, the Buddha. Meet my daughter.
While clouds keep melting into the moon
she is sliding from my arms again.

The Sideways 8

Home from another day of grade one, she says
with a leap in her voice like a swinging gibbon
grabbing a branch, today she learned
                              the biggest number of all.
A billion, her father expects, a trillion,
but she flings her jacket to the floor,
kicks off her boots and shouts, "Infinity!"
Lit up and propelled by the idea, she runs
into the dining room calling, "Infinity! Infinity!"
to the cats sleeping on the placemats.

She laughs as if endlessness were a joke
only a child can get. Returned to her father,
she throws her arms around his knees: "And it looks
like a sideways 8!" Her glance suggests
he's a mathematical dunce, Pater Ignoramus.
Infinity might be a wild Arabian stallion
whose trust she wins slipping sugar cubes
into the wooden pen where he paces.

Sunday, the family follows a path around
a pond, where mallards and mergansers drift among
ice chunks, snow dwindled into the pockets
of permanent shadows. A fallen branch becomes
a walking stick, a staff. Her brother teases,
"Midget wizard." By a brook wide as her mother's stride
she fishes for last fall's residue,
catches a pocked, drenched oak leaf.
"Beautiful," she says of such decay

picked off the stick's end. As the sun keeps up
its meltwater-making, she says the same
of an ice cake her father lifts from the shallows
and holds up high enough for sunlight
to strike — a mass of flashing gems.

Before they finish circling the pond, where turtles'
heartbeats begin to quicken out of hibernation,
she abandons her stick and with one finger
traces in the dark mud along the water
a sign her parents, hand in hand, slowly read.

Breathing and Reading

The father has read the son many books.
   Now in silence the son turns pages,
fingertips pressing the edges of a story

   like a small table across his lap
spread with shells and bones and feathers
   to hold up in the bedside lamplight.

He delves into the silences surrounding
   phrases, the lives that arise
from what's unspoken, twenty-six symbols

   translated into other rooms, other
beds and creatures. He's proud of this newness
   yet not ready to be left alone with it,

so son and father, pillow-propped, cradle
   different books, shoulders and legs touching,
until sleep shuts the page.

   Over the years this pair have traveled
with Joe Otter and his pup, Abraham
   and Isaac, Copperfield and Murdstone,

the woodcarver who forsook his patched coat
   to buy his boy-puppet an ABC book.
From the belly of a shark, a beast

afflicted with heart trouble and asthma,
Pinocchio climbed up to the great mouth
and slipped back into the ocean

with Geppetto hanging from his shoulders.
The father knows nights will come
when the son wants to tumble into sleep alone

so he doesn't budge, he tries to anchor
his mind in his own book,
but hears the faintest unconscious

whispering, then his son's breath rising
and falling, as it rose and fell
in infancy. They divide the hour

like a loaf of bread offered by a stranger
when hunger, cold, and storm
slow their steps far from home.

Now the father only pretends to read:
in rhythm with his heartbeat,
his son's eyes moving from left to right.

For Anyone with a Body

Rushing up stone steps, late, hearing-bound,
          a lawyer hums the first bar of "Body and Soul,"
then reaches down to check his zipper.
                    Cat-called in a seaside park,
     a high-breasted woman with Olympian stride
          glances down at the bounce
under her shirt, while an acne-plagued boy on a bus
     slides closer to a cracked window
to study his reflection, and in stalled
                         post-funeral traffic
     a driver dusts her old cheeks with a powder-puff,
          hiding her tear streaks. The streets
fill with strangers who tweak their ear lobes,
               finger-comb their hair, scratch
     armpits, as if their bodies always
               needed correction.
     Shrug, squirm.
                    In the Neptune Theatre lobby
     a woman pulls her husband's hand
from his mouth, whispering, "You're muffling
                    yourself," and he recalls his mother
     doing the same to his father, as if a need
          to strain words through fingers
     got carried down the generations.
                    Flinch, twitch.
     Some days we'd like to be a cat
sprawling indifferently, obscenely, on a rug in the sun.

Some days we'd embark
on a ship where no mirrors hang
on the cabin walls, where our every motion
says *I am here, undivided,*
perfectly at home —
then we finger the creases
on our foreheads, rub
our elbows, just by our funnybones.

What Happens to Calendars

for Susan Kerslake

In the liveliest room of the Critical Care wing
children make vivid envelopes
out of calendars from past years. They cut,

fold, and glue the months' photos to shape
pockets for letters, then press
adhesive labels with their thumbs.

In this art, January is no better or worse
than June, May favoured no more than December.
The new envelopes are brilliant with

fruit cradled in Mexican pottery, humming-
birds with blue eye-patches or ruby throats,
faces and bicycles in a Chinese market.

At one of the tables, cystic fibrosis holds
three children in its hard arms. It knows their lungs
inside out. Lyle and Yu Ling take scissors

to a butterfly calendar, carefully;
Gretchen chooses wolves — a solitary one staring
into the camera, close up, great-toothed mouth

open wide; two pups gamboling in snow.
The children's eyes are narrowed, intent.
Inside the envelopes, gone days lie hidden

in rows, their penned-in notes fading:
Check wine   X-Ray   Jazz Dance
Bill's b'day   Massage   Call home

Playground, May Day

Shadowless, I am the ghost of the man who planted
    that single tree
two centuries ago. I walk through this spring day unseen,
    hearing all.
High in the mouth of a tube slide, a boy begs his mother
    "Be a dragon,"
while she waits below, open-armed. A blue dragonfly fans
    the toes of a doll
stuck head-first in the sand. Older boys run *up* a slide;
    at the top a young one
puzzles over backwardness. Pigeons — plump trapeze-artists —
    pace around the lip
of a chimney top. I give a girl on a swing a push
    too gentle to be felt,
she draws back her legs and kicks at the sun, her blondeness
    catching in the chains.

By monkey-bars, a father jots in a note-pad while I peer
    over his shoulder:
It's May Day. Remember the summer we stumbled around Europe,
    playground to playground,
missing most galleries? He inhales the smell of fresh bread,
    draws it deep down
into his lungs — *If I owned that bakery, I'd call it* AROMA
    or ENTICEMENT.
His son lifts the pen from his hand, zigzags away.

How many minds here are monkey-bars, how many hearts
    teeter-totters?
"Streets on fire . . . dead civilians," phrases floating
    from a radio
in the lap of a man on a park bench, his face all lines,
    a pacemaker hidden
in his chest. When I rest by him, his cellphone rings —
    out-of-season
grasshopper — and he pulls it from his shirt pocket, mumbles,
    "Who's there?"
I watch three boys hanging from a rusted bar, their legs
    like primate tails,
fizziness popping in their heads, their neighbourhood
    turned on end.
I approach a man in canary shorts and sunglasses
    slumped in grass
studying the numbers on the lottery tickets in his hand.
    I breathe hope into his ear.

Caps shading their faces, two children bury their mother
    in grey pebbles.
Her face — squinting, stranded — struggles out a smile.
    In a bedroom window
a sick girl, groggy and gazing down upon her neighbours,
    imagines them turned
into stone, then brought back to life by the lion Aslan.

It's May Day, but ants leaking from a tree trunk aren't singing
    "The Union Forever."
The sun's falling, the playground abandoned but for me
    and a small gust

of sparrows. Around us the bakery's aroma drifts:
    the bread of the day
risen, mixing more kinds of grain than anyone can count.
    After thousands of miles
at sea, a gull feather spins, tufting a house of sand.
    Underground,
moles quicken along their tunnels, worms open
    breathways for the earth.

Given Words

*Each of us stands on the shoulders of thousands of men
and women who have gone on before us. It isn't just one
hand holding the pen or moving across the keyboard. . . .
The poem written has only a bit of myself in it and far
more of the world.*

— Don Domanski

My Father's Birth

The Telegraph-Journal, November 17, 1925

1

England's greatest cross-country flier is soaring toward Lyons
on the first leg of a flight from London
                                    to Cape Town, by way of Cairo,
aboard a De Havilland 50-plane
                            equipped with a Siddeley Jaguar motor.

The City Cornet Band opened their tenth Around-the-World Fair.
Despite numerous counter attractions,
attendance was large, and everything went with a swing.
Crowds broke into cheers,
factory whistles shrieked a welcome.

Newport Johnny Brown is a hard-hitting, scientific boxer
matched to fight Chick Suggs, champion featherweight.
Newport Johnny is in the pink of condition.

2

WINNIPEG — Met by motor cars,
the visitors were whisked to the Legislature.
In an atmosphere charged with patriotic fervour,
reference was made to the baffling problems,
political and economic, crying for attention.

Children Cry for Fletcher's Castoria —
a pleasant harmless Substitute for Castor Oil,
Paregoric, Teething Drops and Soothing Syrups,
for Infants in arms and Children all ages.

"I do not speak the language of resentment
or bitterness," declared Right Hon. Arthur Meighen.

3

The death of Henry Louis Pierce, aged 12 years,
son of William and Ivy Pierce of Moss Glen.
Funeral, Tuesday afternoon at Chapel Grove.

Joan met them at the gate — her small face startled
in the faint moonlight. "This, I suppose," she said breath-
lessly, "is the end of the story." Peter Lyster looked at Nan.
"No," he said steadily. "It's only the beginning."

Zam-Buk rapidly knits damaged tissues together
and soon removes all traces of injury
by a covering of healthy new skin.

May I not forget
That poverty and riches are of the spirit.
Though the world knows me not,
May my thoughts and actions be such
As shall keep me friendly with myself.
Lift up my eyes from the earth and let me
Not forget the uses of the stars.

The raccoon felt so sure crossing the brook
would be safe, this was a great surprise.
He didn't feel like running and didn't know
where to run to. It wouldn't be safe simply
to climb a tree. Then the dogs would bark at the foot,
and the hunters come over. All of a sudden
it popped into his head —
                    You should have seen him scamper
down along the edge of the Laughing Brook
just in the water. Finally he crossed
to the other side. He was safe.

        4

HORIZONTAL
14. Child
21. Work of skill
27. To ring a bell
29. Name
37. Shooting forth
46. Exclamation of surprise
54. Digit of the foot
61. Portion of the eye
63. Behold

VERTICAL

3. To knock
6. Gazing fixedly
23. Plot of ground
35. Fragrant smell
38. Reverential fear
41. To mimic
50. To breathe
58. Adored
78. Exist

A Short History of Shelters

Daniel March, *Home Life in the Bible*
(Philadelphia: Ziegler & McCurdy, 1873)

1 rock

A few words written on the camel's back
where the tribes began their march into wilderness:

Flocks of goats along hillsides, like black flies
creeping over the white walls of a house.
The sun shot fiery shafts upon the surface
of shining rock and drifted sand. My pulse
beat three strokes for two. The orange I carried
to moisten my lips
                              dried to a husk.

Under the shadow of the great rock
the air was cool. We gathered beneath
and spread our frugal board
                              upon the bare ground.

2 tent

When men expect to live a healthful life
seven hundred years in the same house
gathering riches and local attachments
their thought would be:
                              make everything of earth and time.

The shepherd who saw black tents on the plain
might pass the spot at noon and see nothing
but trampled grass, ashes, tracks of camels.
The wind, a sudden stroke
upon my tent in the early morning,
every stake torn from the earth.

Many of the most beautiful passages
would never have been written
if the home of the tribes had not been tents.

3   *made of mud*

The dwellings of the doves and the people
are all alike in the distance, made of mud
from the Nile. No floor but bare earth, no bed
but such as the jackal finds in the deserted tomb.
The mat was passed through smoke
before it was spread for me to recline upon.

Thirty-three centuries have wrought little change
in the homes in the valley. When a house goes
to ruin, nothing is left
but sun-baked mud.
                              An overflow dissolved
the houses, spread them over the valley
to fertilize the fields.

Cool bright water from my father's well —
I would travel to the far-distant place
of my birth. Be not ashamed of longing
to drink again from the well in whose dark depths
you saw the bucket sink and rise.

Many houses are such we should be ashamed
to call them ours — many make us miserable
if we spend a day within the walls.
The house you now have will soon
pass into other hands. You say, "This is where
I live, these are my acquaintances,
this is the way I spend my life."

In a while your steps will no longer be heard
in the house. You will no longer mingle
in the conversation of those that now
seek your society. The work you are now doing
will be done by others, or not done at all.

So shall the lowliest home be the entrance-chamber.

Head Sketches

A. O'Leary, *The Delineation of Character, As Determined by the Teachings of Phrenology, Physiology, and Physiognomy* (Boston: Bradley, Dayton, 1860)

1 constitution

You want compactness, close-jointedness,
a more sinewy, fibrous texture. Should avoid
scaffoldings and high, dangerous places
lest, in a flush of blood to the head,
you get dizzy. Will be always crippled
for want of the beef and bone of life.

You start too suddenly, stop
too suddenly — need what sailors call ballast.
Exercise as much as you can
short of absolute fatigue.

Something of the wine of life, the wild berry wine.

2   *mentality & memory*

Thick-thoughted, blunt, you could sit
an hour thinking of nothing
or rather
not thinking of anything.

If people's names were printed on their forehead
so you could read them every time
you look in their faces, you would have
a very fair memory of names.
You sometimes forget, for a moment,
your own name.

You often say, "I would give the world to know,"
in an affair that would be worth
half the world at most.

3   *expressiveness*

Disposed to interjectional
expressions — *Oh, my! Ah! Indeed! Strange!*

When excited, you speak faster than your words
come, and hence you hesitate
and hang on to the one just spoken, waiting
for the next impatiently, and appearing to
stammer, endeavouring
to catch it before you can.

4   *aesthetics*

A thunderstorm is to you little more
than a thunderstorm, so much rain,
so much wind. Would rather sacrifice
the rose to the cabbage.
Are not wanting in a taste for poetry
but the glitter covers it.

You may catch glimpses of the ideal life
but all in all your imagination is plain,
your fancy tame. Cultivate Constructiveness
by taking an interest in machinery,
playing chess and draughts.

5   *four arrows*

Your aftersight better than your foresight.

More likely to rust out than wear out.

Your laugh is light, not deep or hearty.

Little real kindness, little real cruelty.

6 *the future*

Cannot well tell a fool from a philosopher,
nor a rogue from either. Profit
by engaging in business that would throw you
into contact with strangers,
                              and by reading carefully
the master-daguerrotypists of the soul.

In new countries, deep forests, or on the water,
apt to be lost and bewildered,
turned around. Have not intuitive knowledge
of the compass. Death will find your door
open, or at least ajar.
What's the hurry? Eternity is long.

You seek the home as the beast does
his lair, to lie down and rest.
Sleep all you can, for in sleep
is your only safety.

London, in the Beginning

F. Hopkinson Smith, *In Dickens's London*
(New York: Charles Scribner's Sons, 1914)
G.E. Mitton, *The Thames*
(London: Blackie and Son, 1910)

1

Nooks and cracks and crannies
through which you can hardly squeeze your way
with a wheelbarrow, let alone a cab or hansom —

Along the Great Embankment
where the stone-and-iron monsters wade knee-deep
in the Thames, their broad backs freighted with multitudes —

2

A continuous wabble from sill to eaves, its roof-line
sagging, its chimney out of plumb, shorter flues
climbing up taller ones as if struggling
for air, the wonder being that it had not long ago
lost all heart.
        A landlady peered at me
through the panes of a low-sashed window, shouted
to the boot cleaner in the waistcoat with blue glass buttons.

Eager men fringed the lunch counters, barmaids
shunting beer into this mug and that Toby;

breathless clerks grabbed a sandwich, smeared its inside
with mustard, shot over to the cigar stand.

Big fiddle-back chairs with or without arms;
a very old clock as big as a coffin
and shaped the same.

3

The order for regulation of the swans
runs to thirty clauses, a quaint document.
The Thames swans belong to the Crown,
the Vintners' and Dyers' Companies. So ancient
are the rights in this matter that their origin
is lost in antiquity. *Swan-hopping* is really
swan-upping, the process of taking up the swans
to mark them according to ownership.

The well-known tavern sign THE SWAM WITH TWO NECKS
is a corruption of THE SWAM WITH TWO NICKS.

4

Into my cab once more along Covent Garden
and Henrietta Street, into a publishing house
smelling of printer's ink, hot glue, and leather.
The desks, tables and chairs made in year one,
the mahogany kept bright by a line of editors,
proofreaders, and editors going back to the Paleozoic Age.

5

All I had to do was drop
in my two and six

and out would come a licence
permitting me to walk over as many graves

as I liked between twelve and four.

The Breeze Made Such Music

Rowland E. Prothero, *The Psalms in Human Life*, 4th edition
(London: John Murray, 1914)

In memory of Hubert Bartlett

1

There is scarcely a leaf in the Psalter
not stained by some withered flower.
To gather some of these petals and read —

Above the couch of David hung a harp. The midnight breeze
made such music that the poet-king was constrained
to rise from his bed, and till dawn
he wedded words to the strains.

2

The hart (Psalm 42: 1), emblem of thirsting souls
gathered in the catacombs of great cities —
wool-workers, cobblers, craftsmen, slaves.
The ploughman carolled them over his furrow,
the carter hummed them by his wagon.
Ancient trade guilds found the legend
of their charter: "Thou has put all things in subjection
under his feet" (The Butchers' Company).

To coins they furnished legends —
florin of Edward III, shilling of Edward VI,
coin struck to commemorate the execution of Charles I.

On the shores of Stranford Lough,
Columba became a pupil of St. Finnian. Legend tells us
he copied his host's psalter by stealth,
shutting himself up by night where the book was treasured
and writing by the light which streamed from his own hand.

On the Psalms, as his mother repeated them,
James Hogg nursed his imagination
and mingled with them her tales of giants, kelpies,
brownies, and other aerial creations.

After he stood on the scaffold
midst the instruments for torture
William Wallace begged Lord Clifford
to restore his psalter. The prayer was granted.
Unable to hold the book
in his chained hands, he asked a priest
to keep it open for him, and as he hung
from the gallows, still sensible, disemboweled,

he remained fixed upon it until his eyes closed.

Sword blades, truncheons and rings, sundials
all over the world: "My days are gone like a shadow."

No book relies less upon forms of opinion to which
the ages have given their transitory mould.

No words come home to us with swifter, surer flight.
The lyrical burst of tenderness, broken accents
of shame and penitence, oil of gladness.
The hart.   The hart.

What He Chose to Record

The diaries of C.B. (Crawford Buntin) Lawrence, written 1889-1918

1 a few rhymes from a life

hauled 5 hogsheads of herring   plowed down to Russells
put in cellar wall   pedelled cider and appels

hauled rockweed and sod and mixed them for potatoes
hauled load of straw from Joes   helped Joe build tables

took Mother to town   thinned turnips   went to Lodge
hauled 38 lbs of turnips to Heart & Greenlaws

mended shoes   delivered school bills   chored about barn
hauled load ceeder trees to Sir William Van Horn

put window frame in Fathers room   killed four rackoons
Crismos   went a scating in the afternoon

helped Sam MacFarlane mov hous acrost Lake
hauled 8 stakes to Chamcook for Bismark Dick

sold horse for hundred dollars   received fifteen cash
heavy Hail storm   broke four pains glass

Newton and I walked east side of Limeburner Lake
Sunday   several people called   Father veary sick

worked in Scemetary   finished harvesting grain
went to town for Doctor and brought him home again

Mr Maiders first sermon after Church sheathed
brot home 150 pounds of Bug Death

hewed sled runners   shingled shed   mixed shells
cut load logs and hauled to Bartletts mill my self

Sunday   Minnie and I went to shore   Hot weather
received inlarged Pictures of Father and Mother

repaired fence east of house and brought in last of hay
went to Red Beach to circus   took black cow away

2 going to town

plowed in burnt land and went to town   went to town with
pig carrots beets Cabage   went to town to get Andie Smith
casket   went to town with Minnie and ploughed in the afternoon
went to town and had two teath out   went to St Stephens
for piping for sink   went to town for Mr Groucher who preached
in morning   Mother died at one oclock thirty this morning
went to town and then Oke Bay to see Mr Todd about attend-
ing funeral   Minnie and I went to town to have her tooth
out   went to St Stephens for stove   went to St. Stephens
bought Organ for church   went to town with pigs pork   went
to St Stephens to go to California   Girls went to town for
lessons   went to St Stephens and had seven teeth out   drove to
St Stephens three doctors examined Minnie   Minnie went to

Hospittle I came home   telephone dispatch from hawspittle
    Minnie E Lawrence my Whife
                                        went to town to see CPR
cars   hurt my arm went to town to get it sowed up   drove to
town to tell Parents of James Mallock and Hurbie Williamson
they were drowned   went to town with strawberries and to see
soldiers   went to town sent an order for life insurance

3 *more biography with verbs*

repaired cowstable floor   cleaned out
water clawset   greased harness   hauled
cord wood to Sherif Stewart   took John Wren
over river   topdressed ground for potatoes
salted pig   made drag for hauling turnips
out of cellar   broake roads   split ice
from Vessel   brought Bull out to Bayside   put up
telephone poles   took white faced cow away

to two funerals
to Ministers Island   horse served
by Sir Adam McAdam

went to Oke Point for sheep   did not get any
went to Chamcook for meal   did not get any

cultervated ~~turnips~~ carrots
to pick nick   was on jury   was sick
had to stay in house
    "   "
    "   "
    "   "

62

ground covered in six inches of snow
went for cattle   did not get them
went for cattle with dogs   did not get them

Jips had Colt by Sir Adam McAdam
horse owned by Sir William Van Horn

all went fishing
mended shues
Squallie   Blowed veary heavy, Trees in full blume

C.B. Lawrence, ca. 1890

Minnie Lawrence, ca. 1895

C.B. Lawrence and his children (Georgie on far left, Hermon in back), ca. 1915

Early Readings, 1908

The New Brunswick Readers: Third Book
"prescribed by the Board of Education for New Brunswick"
(Toronto: W. J. Gage & Company, 1900)

The pimpernel is not the only weather prophet.
If you go into the garden and find the African marigold
shut after seven o'clock in the morning,
you may be sure
there will be a rainy day.
                    The boy knew it by a feeling
in his veins — a spring stir in his arms and legs
which tempted him to stand on his head
                        or throw a handspring
if he could find a spot of ground
from which the snow had melted.

Again I started the heavy load, and struggled on
a few yards; again the whip came down
and again, forward. That great cartwhip was sharp,
my mind hurt as much as my poor sides.
            Here was a moment for Miner Jack and Miner Will.
Instant death hangs over them. Will generously
resigns himself. "Go aloft, Jack. Away!
In one minute I shall be in — "

Aladdin was terrified to find himself buried alive.
He cried out, and called to his uncle
offering to give him the lamp, but too late.
He happened to rub the ring: out of the earth
an enormous genius in whose hand

was a torch that lighted up the cave
as though the sun —
                              She lighted another
and now was sitting under the most splendid tree,
larger than the one seen through the window
at the rich merchant's. She stretched out both hands
just as the match burnt out.
He thought I was a ghost, mother, for I was all in white,
and I ran by him without speaking like a flash of light.
They call me cruel-hearted, but I care not what they say,
for I'm to be Queen o' the May, mother, I'm to be —

Nothing broke the silence of the night
but the gurgling river and the low voice of Wolfe:
he repeated stanzas of Gray's "Elegy,"
just received from England. "Gentlemen,"
he said, as he closed his recital,
"I would rather have written those lines
than take Quebec tomorrow."
                              Said Jim Baker,
"There's more to a blue jay than to any other
creature. He has more kinds of feeling;
and whatever a blue jay feels
he can put into words. No common words either,
but out-and-out book talk. Never a jay
at a loss for a word."

The children used to come down in long bright slanting rows
and say all together, "Who is this in pain?"
When I told them who I was,
they answered, "Come play with us."
When I said, "I never play! I can't play!"
they swept about me and took me up and made me light.

Dear Georgie

Letters written in October 1918 by Hermon Lawrence
of Bayside, New Brunswick to his older sister, Georgie
Bartlett, while he was training in the 3rd Heavy Canadian
Battery, Composite Bridge, Witley Camp, Surrey, England

The war news have been good for quite awhile
but I dont think it can be fought
to a finish this fall.

I havent yet got that box you mailed Aug 10
and was about giving it up until today
when Tom Walker told me he just received

a box mailed July 7th, a jar of strawberries in it.
They hadnt put the wire clip over the cover —
well the strawberries had run all through

and spoiled it. A shame to throw it all away.
The first of the week I saw a play,
"Lucky Durham." The main thing is to have

the parts well acted. I suppose I wont
be satisfied to see moving pictures.
Plays will be apt to spoil me.

I heard a fine illustrated lecture on Pompeii,
Rome and Naples. The lecturer had a lantern
with slides, views all down the west coast of Italy,

Vesuvius. Nearly all the beauty of Europe
isnt natural, but the work of man. Very different
from the beauty of America. I want to see

more of America, if I can arrange to
without too much trouble.
The Hotels Cecil and Savoy on the Strand

are the best hotels in London. I wasnt in them
but on the grounds around them.
I would like to spend about 24 hours

in one. When we get to our new camp
we will all have heavy horses.
The worst part is cleaning the harness,

all the steel will have to be kept shining.
One is apt to have a few tumbles at first
over the jumps. The weather changes very quick —

one can never tell in the morning what kind of day
it will be. Oh how are the apples this year.
Have they had a very large crop.

Sometimes I sit in one of the chairs
in front of the fireplace — they have been keeping
a fire lately — and go over the times we had

in my mind. I would like to farm just as we did
but there will have to be some change.
It wont do for Dwight and I to go on working

together. That will have to be settled later.
The first thing for me to take a hand in settling
is this business over here.

Hermon Lawrence, 1918

Georgie Bartlett, 1916

My Mother's Birth

The Telegraph-Journal, December 15, 1928

1

LONDON — King George's Physicians issued
the bulletin: "The King had a disturbed day
and the general condition is not quite
satisfactory. The pulse, however, remains steady."

MOSCOW — Two whitened skeletons, the separate skulls
grinning against a background of virgin snow,
have solved the 20-year mystery surrounding
the polar expedition of Roald Amundsen.

A new record for activity was established
in today's trading, largely through the turnover
in International Nickel, which soared into new high ground.

The general list moved in a distinctly buoyant manner.

2

Ever so many dolls to choose from, even if
purchase was limited to one precious dollar.

Ranged in size from a tiny person one could
hide under a stamp — at least a Special Delivery Stamp —

to a large fat baby doll with a mild expression,
all of twelve inches high. A careful selection

must be made — dark hair or light, blue eyes
or brown, corn-coloured frocks, rose and apple green.

   3

The morning of the snow, Mother read them a bit
about Maggie and Tom in "The Mill on the Floss":

"Snow lay on the croft and river bank
in undulations softer than the limbs of infancy —

Old Christmas meant to light up home
with new brightness, deepen the riches of indoor colour."

Franz Schubert left $10 worth of clothes
and a thousand melodies. Impossible to say

what became of his clothes, but the melody lingers.
One of the earliest carol makers was Wynken de Worde,

who flourished in the sixteenth century,
who composed the carol in honour of the boar's head.

Gone the boar's head, replaced by the stuffed turkey
and gone the old carol to make way for the new.

4

Jingle of pots and pans, clashing like cymbals.
Hot tallow, scorched cedar, pungent orange peel
and the tang of paint on new wooden toys. The new moon
dropping down the west, a frosted feather.
The windows of every home, sharp-cut squares of glory.
The star, making sparkles on the weather vane.

"Do you remember the young lady who engaged you
last Saturday?" "Yes, sir."
"Well, where did you put her down?"
The taxi man scratched his head.
"Why, the Royal Planet Hotel."

The bells exercise a spell. They awaken
rhythm and music not sensed at other times.
The best within us awakens with the first pealing of these bells.

First Lessons in Symbiosis

Sigmund A. Lavine, *Strange Partners*,
a children's book of natural history
(Boston: Little, Brown & Company, 1959)

While other residents of the Great Barrier Reef
shun the stinging, lasso-like tentacles
of the *Discosoma*,
                        clownfish swim in and
out of the death-dealing threads. At night
when the anemone closes up, the fish rests
inside, safe. In return for this protection
clownfish not only clean the insides of their partners
but also massage the tentacles.

No longer does any country have to fight
disease, fire, flood, illiteracy, and starvation alone.

Oysters gladly supply shelter for oyster crabs
for these tiny creatures, scavengers,
pay their rent by removing waste
that would make their landlords uncomfortable.

Do you make a fuss when asked to take care
of your younger brothers and sisters?

The brave dentist who enters the broad snout
of the largest living reptile
is a species of plover. Even harmless protozoa
in the human alimentary tract
earn the food and warmth given them.

That is why men of all nations and faiths
signed the United Nations Charter.

The angler fish is shaped like a misformed globe.
A third of its length: a massive head containing
a tremendous mouth. Growing out of its head
is a filament ending in a light organ
just like a swaying Japanese lantern.
Luminous bacteria reside in the tip.

Fragments from 2073 AD

Dr. G. Hartwig, *The Polar and Tropical Worlds:
A Description of Man and Nature in the Polar
and Equatorial Regions of the Globe*
(Springfield, Mass.: Bill, Nichols & Co., 1873)

1

Iceland might as well be called Fireland.

Anchoring to an iceberg is not always
unattended with danger, particularly
when summer is far advanced.
Dr. Hayes witnessed the crumbling of an immense berg
resembling the British Houses of Parliament.

Cairns of stone point the way,
small huts erected as a refuge. Houses and ships
used to be built of indigenous timber.
The dwarf shrubberies here and there are not
to be dignified with the name of woods.

As coal is too expensive, the majority
make use of dried cow's and sheep's dung,
but many a poor fisherman lacks even this
and is fain to use the bones of animals,
the skeletons of fishes or dried seabirds.

2

The natives were treated with cruelty
and blood flowed in torrents
to keep up the prices of cloves and nutmegs.
When these spices accumulated
in too large a quantity, they were thrown into the sea
or destroyed by fire.

Its bite causes an intolerable itching
which drives by day the perspiration of anguish
from every pore, and at night makes one's hammock
the gridiron on which Saint Lawrence was roasted.

They say it is dangerous to eat,
but what is a hungry man to do?

3

Not infrequently strangers land
and leave not a single egg behind.
Blood, of which not a drop is lost, is drunk
warm, or made into black pudding.
Bones and hooves serve for excellent glue.
Eggs and oily flesh of seabirds
furnish a miserable food for infants.

Ginklofi: rolling of eyes, cramps, lockjaw,
the back bent like a bow, either backward
or forward. The only means of preserving infants:
send them to the mainland to be reared.

4

Few settlements separated by immense deserts
give proof of weak attempts
to establish   a footing.
We come from the unknown, and plunge
                              into the unknown.

Here we seek in vain that variety of insects,
the clamorous voices that resound in thickets.

Fox in this country is all bone and hair.

Breathing and Reading

Thumbnail Biographies

1

A wolf nursed him in the woods when he was nameless.
He grew lithe as an otter, hands fast enough to catch
rabbits on the run. A bear-trap broke his ankle.
Pulled by horse and sled to a distant town, he learned
a language that swallowed his whistles and growls.
Women coached him to make butter,
men to hammer iron. Fire was the new animal
he loved best. The word "love" was a ball of mud
revolving in his mouth as he hugged the knees
of the pastor's daughter. Her father thought him
a devil, but she loved his furred ears and hands
so they fled to another country where they grew
old together, weaving carpets and baskets
from riverside reeds. Wolves circling his grave
rubbed their noses against his tombstone.

2

His mother's braided black hair. Cold white scales.
Gentian-blue blanket, plaid perambulator,
his father's hazel eyes. First purple bruise.
First fear of black night. Greens
of baseball grass-stains on his shirt
and knees, greens of the trail-eating
forest, the deep sea. Violet dress,
a gold chain between breasts. Black hair

of his daughter's wet head: first sight of her.
Multi-coloured bits of a kaleidoscope,
a gift from his six children. Navy-blue suits
to work, orange PJs for a joke.
Pink of small pills dissolving
on his tongue to calm him. Silver
wings of planes that carried his grown children
away. Fuzzing of colours as his eyes
dimmed, yellow of phlegm coughed up
in old handkerchiefs. Northern Lights
the last time he turned his head on a pillow
to see what the Venetian blinds were cutting up.

3

She was born five minutes after her sister
who only lived one minute. Her mother disappeared
like a mouse in the pantry. Her grandparents
notched her growth on an oak doorframe.
Strong-lunged long-distance swimmer,
she never read the news, but fans kept scrapbooks,
the heroine always in a bathing cap. Her name
swam into record books before she gave birth
to twins, called them April and June
because her sister had been May for a minute.
In their teens her carpenter husband made
matching bookends, a mermaid's face and tail
carved from maple, but when he abandoned her
for a skier, she buried the bookends in her garden.
Thanks to a transplanted heart, she lived into
her sixties. Forgotten by all but few,

she went on walks every day, Mozart or Miles
in her earphones, until early one morning
in the Public Gardens she folded onto
her knees, then clutched her sister's ankle
in the waters opening around her on all sides.

West End, Halifax

In this moist corner
   of a used-book store
a lone mushroom sprouts

             Two giant zucchini
                by a grinning girl's ears —
             green parenthesis

He holds high his rolled-up
   Yoga mat, fending off
a crow diving close

             The blackout lasts
                one second — the neighbourhood
             blinks — glimpse of Zilch

Where Dublin St. meets
    London St., a soaked atlas
falls apart in grass

Behemoth tree-trimmer spits
    limbs into its gut —
noisiest eater around

Garbage night, one hopeful
    sound in the dark —
bottle-scavengers' bags clink

From under ice
    in a mid-winter thaw
a worm crawls, earth's colour

A sort of grace —
    a falling icicle strikes
his foot, not his eye

          Blizzard-buried,
             a locked bicycle's shrunken
          to its red reflector

A maple wingseed
    stays stuck to a skate blade
crisscrossing a rink

          Two bootprints frozen
             in sidewalk ice, one pointing
          down the street, one up

Through twelve months
   a scarecrow on a porch gives
each season the same scowl

                         Oh for X-rays to show
                            all the tree roots holding
                         these streets together

Ninety Crows in the Backyard

for Rose Adams

Abrupt visitants — voices raw as those of creatures protesting
the flaying of their flesh, as morphed bat-squeaks upped many
decibels and pushed down into baritone and bass — pull me
to the window to part the sheers and face blacknesses gathering
in the bare treetops just now starting to bud in early spring,
where summer, fall, and winter are also seasons of the crow,
bird worthy to bless a family crest: *Hardiness.*

One whose name even the least avian-minded know, nursery-
rhyme and folk-tale favourite, this bird — present to the full
— thrives between past and future, between a neighbour's glass
windchimes and the moose-bellow of a distant ship's horn.
Air-tumbler, wind-surfer, sparrow-frightener. At first a dozen,
then double that, the colour of coal or basalt, half the phrase *crow
black*, source of the *Canadian Oxford* noun meaning *a happy or
triumphant cry uttered by a person*, person like him who rambles
on recalling the complaint *too damn many crow-poems*, then
the dozen is tripled, winter-tested branches bending under the
weight of so many. Morning bird wrapped in bands of night,
afternoon bird rolled in road tar or volcanic ash, night bird
sporting the perfect camouflage.

No effete songster like a Byzantium ornament this one, golf-
ball thief reclaiming the green for the winged, gobbler at the
shore and sentinel over the meadow and floater through falling
snow, harsh cougher, leaf-kicker, calling from the tree tops *Too
many people-poems, too many people-poems.* The tripled dozen
now doubled, splashes of black paint flung by Jackson Pollock,

nothing but birds of gloom and doom to the past-bound yet
cracking the air with calls my ears hear as the rude flipside to
eulogies: a mourner by an opening in the earth gets distracted
by a brash voice and turns to watch the raggedy bird he loves
best, bit-player in more than a thousand memories, bird of
twenty-four hours and twelve months, there, and here, where I
turn away from the window, nourished by corvid health.

Spiders Magnified

Day-old O's the colour of pale earth, smaller
than infants' fingernails, pulse and jiggle
by the dozens, against the sunny side of the house,
just within reach. Day-old legs, snipped threads,
cling, near a bird's streaky smear. Eager cluster,
bewildered digits: blind to what they'll spin and spawn.

When we found this nursery entangled in sunlight
I rushed indoors, pulled the magnifying glass
from the mini-drawer in the foxed slipcase
of our two-volume *Oxford English Dictionary*.

We've guided that glass over *barlafumble, downsteepy,*
boonfellow, wink-a-peep, over words'
threads and webs —
                              but what's this turbulence
outside any script we know?
Fingerprinted, my drugstore reading glasses
double the barrier. How many layers
can you layer to see something, until
it becomes nothing?

Inches distant, oceans distant. We peer across
to arachnid island. I arrest my son's hand as it reaches
for the swarming newborn.

Saint Mary's U Études

in memory of Terry Whalen and Cyril Byrne

1 on teaching with a cold

Since bad blues and a hard-drinking father
hold him down, Ray wears a hood in class,
his jowls stubbled, a bottle of water
locked in his hand, his bitten lips sealed fast.
Maggie, who told me she can't pay her rent,
announces from her desk in the front row,
"What I just said isn't what I meant."
I'm on the edge of saying *Isn't that so
whenever we open our mouths?* when Ray
retreats an inch farther into his hood.

Despite a scratchy throat, the drizzly day,
our conversation dragging like slow blood,
I keep hoping at least one phrase or line
matches Ray's heartbeat, a perfect rhyme.

2   *on teaching* The Tempest

Last week hot curses empurpled the air:
Hang, cur! Hang, you whoreson, insolent noise-
maker! But this week we're into Act IV
where sorrows and guilt deepen, like a voice
thickening as feelings become more mixed.
The fates must laugh since here in Halifax
windows steam up with tempestuous rain
while Beth in the back row reads, *Sir, I am vexed.*
Bear with my weakness, Prospero's pain
silencing his pride, transforming his speech.

. . . *dainty Ariel*, he says, subdued, grief-tugged,
I shall miss thee. It's easier to teach
A pox o' your throat, you blasphemous dog!
What's most tender is most out of reach.

"In my mind it's spray-painted red and blue,"
Rob tell us, then he quotes: *I'm Nobody!*
Who are you? Are you — Nobody — Too?
A few days ago, who thought we'd study
what it means to be *Public — like a Frog?*
Last night's Oscar regalia and hairdos
made Sophie remember *admiring bog*;
she sees how life shrunken to cheers and boos
is the fate of too many Somebodies.
"I'm glad to be one of the Nobodies,"
she says with gusto that lightens my noon
with its A+ to anonymity.
She gives me the faith to ask everyone
to search through Emily for more graffiti.

4   on teaching Poe's "The Fall of the House of Usher"
     the 12th time

Through many years in many rooms I taught
that shadowed story thick with atmosphere
and *unredeemed dreariness of thought*,
frail Usher battling miasmas of fear.
After my first surge of true-blue panic —
trapped-sparrow heart,
                         heaving, attacked breath —
brought me to my knees, broken Roderick
grew vivid, though anthologized to death.
In class I'm tempted to say, "I've been there —
known *the tottering of lofty reason
on her throne.*"
                  Discretion? — or do I dare
leave Poe's pages and recall my wheezing,
weigh words carefully to tell how Usher
is now less a freak, a bit more my brother.

From the ceiling a dead poet slides down
a great liana of vine, then, pant cuffs
cobwebby after three years underground,
he lands feet-first on a desk. The class sluffs
off sleepiness and listens: *I talk*
like a dog, laugh like a man, bark like God!
Desk-walking Al booms Lawrence's "The Snake,"
then pulls out from his bursting sleeve a wad
of poems — or is it a bucket of grapes?
"Was Ameliasburg your second home,
poems your first?" Al lets out a chortle-groan,
answers by reading poem after poem,
then tosses paper cups around the room
and pours purple milk from a jeroboam.

6 *transcendental graffiti*

> I would write on the lintels of the door-post, *Whim*.
> I hope it is somewhat better than whim at last, but
> we cannot spend the day in explanation.
>
> — Emerson

On the inside door frame of a Men's Room
some witty student has scrawled with a pen
one clear black word, Waldo Emerson's *whim*,
a word that makes the mouth purse and open
into a small Aeolus. In these old halls
where priests once took note of blacklisted books
lean, sharp-faced ghosts go floating through the walls
to skewer Waldo's style, all knots and hooks,
parables and paradox. What student
stopped here to transcribe the four-letter word?
It's impossible to say if he meant
to rib the revolutionary of Concord —
or, just as whimsically, aimed a dart
at all who separate living from art.

7   *on skating after teaching Avison's*
     "Butterfly Bones; or Sonnet Against Sonnets"

Alone in the rink — maker of echoes —
you lace up your skates, shake from your shoulders
the deadlines and lists gathered there like crows.
Wrist pains. Ibuprofen. Getting older.
Yet you revel in your speed, your long stride,
the way the air takes your bent-low curving
around corners. Are sonnets *cyanide*
jars? Rigid trophies? Soaring, swerving,
recall sonnets packed with vigour, the heave
of Avison's lines: *patience, learning, leave*
all living stranger. Sweat has quickly
soaked your shirt. Like a solo in bebop,
whizzing past scuffed boards, your scarf pulled free:
fourteen times around the rink non-stop —

Far from her family and home in Glace Bay
a shy girl lifts her hand and volunteers
while those to her left and right glance away
as if asked to confess their deepest fears.
Flushing, blinking, she begins with a soft cough:
The art of losing isn't hard to master....
Launched like a boat downriver, she's off,
giving us the words — *keys, realms, disaster,*
gesture — as if they were her own to give.
Her pacing, perfect. Her ear, sure. Each lift
and dip of her voice suggest she's lived,
beyond her eighteen years, a century.
Does she know it's a gift, this euphony?
"One Art" held in the breath of Stephanie.

Correcting Page Proofs While a Catbird Sings

On page 10, change *blue bandanna* to *red bandanna.*
(Shocked to find *blue* six times
                                        in the first dozen poems.)
Thanks for telling me I've misspelled *killdeer*
all these years, with just one *l.* Was I backing off
from the murder in the second *l?* I click
a Dr. Grip pen, pain piercing my thumb.
Those clicks can't keep up
with the catbird who's chosen
this morning of all mornings to lasso the house:
flute and piccolo notes, mews and
snaps, mellifluousness and harshness all
balled up together.
                        That song's a call to open
the windows wider — I do. Change *echo over*
to *echo across,* even if that loses trochaic ease,
because *over* sounds too lofty, and *across* gives
the horizontal drive I want — echoes
sailing back across a pond.
(Excuse the Lapsang Souchong ring on page 75.)

Hyphens *aren't* weeds, so throw away that herbicide,
spare my two-words-made-one. But thanks
for suggesting *reach to* become *reach for* — there's more
yearning in *for,* isn't there?
                        Catbird's an underdog;
one guide calls its song *a squeaky, grating travesty*
of mockingbird's and thrasher's, but I welcome
anyone so maligned yet so spirited.

The Canadian Oxford says *bannister* can have one *n*
or two, so please put back the missing one. I like *bannister*
with two *n*'s because that way the ride down
is longer and wilder, like Catbird's voice
carrying on and on until it hits the floor of the morning.

Poems Among the Ads

Why am I up here, wonders a poem on a bus,
rubbing shoulders with cat-named cars
and sticks to suppress body smells?
It wants to be built like a canoe, breathe
true, pungent odours — crushed ginger, forgotten
potatoes at the back of a cupboard.
As sunlight plays checkers on its face
it squints. Nagged by self-doubts, it thinks
How can I be a voice crying in the wilderness,
a Cézanne-in-words
up here among the fried chicken and jeans?
It has its pride, this poem, so it squirms
when anyone reads it, emits
a sigh of relief when nobody stands near.
All night in the Central Transit garage
the poem stays awake, plotting
the day it will disguise itself as a passenger
and disembark at the edge of town.

Down the aisle another poem — eavesdropper,
explorer, suffering fools gladly — opens
its white spaces to passengers'
laughter, whispery music from headphones, all
surprise greetings and curt farewells,
kisses of chapped lips. This poem concocts
jokes about being neighbours
with tissues named after a swan, a brand of beer
featuring a great-antlered animal's head.
While the bus lurches, brakes, and begins

again, this poem feels most itself
when someone sitting with a box in her lap
lifts her eyes above the windows and, startled
as if by prism-divided light, reads it.

Time, Flying

Grieving Mountain

in memory of A.R. Ammons

I strolled up to the mountain and gave it
sad news: "The man who talked with you

was buried today, and many mourn —
though more would weep for a president

or a pop star." Brooks rushed and rattled
faster, the mountain's mouthpiece: "I liked

talking to him too, he made little poems
with me in them, not the big ones

you'd expect. I get tired of awed
gazes and apostrophes, so I was glad

when he chatted as if I were an acorn.
Sometimes we just want to be ant hills. . . .

But here I'm running off
at the mouth, as I never did with him."

The sunlight was so strong I shaded
my eyes with one hand: "Grief does that,

grief loosens the tongues of mountains."
"Oh yes," the mountain said, backed up by

woodpeckers and wind, "though I should skip
rather than weep. If anyone understood that,

the comic psalmist did." "Why is it,"
I asked, "you were pithier with him?"

The mountain darkened: "Don't think
for a moment I'd talk to you the way

I talked to him." Then quietness
fell around us both until, abashed,

I asked, "Anything else you want told
back among the gaggle of poets?"

But the mountain, silent, only rained
cones down around my boots.

One Minute on a Planet

1

Deep in a cave dark as an ocean floor, nothing
crawls or flits, squeaks or whirrs. The cool air

never grows warmer or cooler, no matter
what changes outside. A lantern-toting traveller

might say those walls hold space without time,
a chamber of absolute waiting, a fore-world.

Lampless, anyone would be blind,
blackness like an all-consuming pupil;

even some tombs are livelier,
granted decomposition. Silence is complete

but for the waterdrop splashing on rock,
mocking time. There, painter and poet

have no business. There a barefoot print
rests in sand, flower-fresh, for a thousand years.

2

Across an island all feathers and noise
  mobs of jammed-together bodies and a riot of wings
    lift off the ground, stir up
  a high-pitched wind. Hovering kittiwakes
moan, gannets gaggle, herring gulls riddle
  the bright air with cries. Heat-split,
    rotten eggs pop. Feet like flattened lizards
  settle onto rocks and algae, ledges and pinnacles,
regurgitated eels, all shades of guano.
  A cormorant dumps a pellet of exoskeletons
    onto its mate's foot; a younger one plunges
  its head far down a parent's throat, hunger a piston.
Klepto black-backed gulls tug gannets' catches
  from their mouths. Puffins in long rows grip herring
    in their carnival beaks, not dropping one
  until a ripple of reverberant pressure
nudges them all. A trampled, crevice-trapped
  murre chick lifts its head, shivers
    with a spasm. Only in death does it slide
  into silence, the silence between
splashes of water in a distant cave.

Travels of the Watch

1

Like the cat mistaken for a fur hat, the watch
likes to travel, more faithful than any bracelet.
Each day it whispers thanks it isn't a clock
hooked to a wall, parked on a shelf. In the garden,
sweat slicks it on one side, marigold dust
gathers on the other;
                    at the seaside it sprawls
on a jaguar-faced towel from Copacabana, edgy
about sand grains. Minutes bake inside its shell.
Like a bird on a hippo's back, a mite
in a bird's feathers, it goes along for the ride.

Even on days when it never leaves the house
invading sunlight reflects off its face, casting
jumpy spots
                on the floors and walls.
That dance is the greatest freedom it knows
strapped to a wrist.

2

On the watchmaker's table, exposed,
its cogs and wheels
quiver, hoping to spring up
and fly like a swarm of insects,

a noiseless blur of parts
in the face of Fate.

3

Half the time its owner forgets to slip it off
for the night, so it taps its tiny drum
in the dark near her pulse, that subtler time-keeper.
But before she makes love, she unstraps it
and drops it on her bedside table, by peach pits
or flaming candles. As its band's tarnish
fades, it feels young again: the woman
sails across an ocean beyond all minutes and days.

While she and her man breathe like sea lions
the watch plays. It makes the hour hand go
fast as the second hand, the second hand slow
as the hour. Nothing of her clings to it
but one grey hair. Stretching between a glass of wine
and a nine-hundred-page novel, the watch
lolls — yet can't banish the metronome
in its palace of interlocked silver. Even the watch
grows tired of time and wishes it could
unstrap itself,
                    cast itself off,
sustained by some other heartbeat.

The Verdict

One of those waking-you-up-breathless,
whipping-the-horses-of-your-heartbeat
nightmares . . . but a quiet dream, the drama
underplayed, under the skin, caught
in a bland room where I was sent to prison.

At breakfast, I can't recall the crime,
if I was guilty or innocent. Someone I know
(friend? sibling?) touched my shoulder:
"Only eighteen months." I have no memory
of judge or jury, only the verdict.
                              Lung-filling panic
told me I live less in months and years
than in minutes and hours. I felt like the first man
doomed never to wake up again to daylight
in his window, tree shadows falling over his face.

Those eighteen months stretched to the horizon,
each day a nail under my bare foot.
The spoon in my hand shakes under judgment.

Damn Clock

Polished golden stones surrounded its twelve hours
    like sun rays — but its first morning in the house
I banished it to the hall closet. It was a loud clock,
    a clock that beat out time like a migraine
pulse, the clicks of a treadmill turned
    by a hypnotized rat. I did not want silence
punctuated so, did not want my morning
    measured out by a metronome, cut up into its
14,440 seconds.

That night she said, "You'll get used to it"
    (and yes, I could learn to block out
my amplified heartbeat broadcast
    in quadrophonic sound). With its perfectly
paced, battery-fed clicks, more tedious
    than the steadiest rain, it could learn a lesson
from the junco in the backyard, who strings out
    his simple trill, yet goes silent when enough
is enough. That night, I'd hardly settled
    into the tub's high waters when I heard it
again, dripping-tap-imitator, now stationed
    on the bathroom counter, counting out seconds
like bent galley slaves sweating and whipped,
    keeping the oars to their ruthless rhythm.

In the morning, in the kitchen, radio voices
    grew louder, then softer, slowed down,
speeded up. While the day chanted
    its soundless mantra, I eyed
the twelve-stoned face on the windowsill.

Time, Flying

1

A day per page, one dark number, bolder
than thirty-one lined up in rows
like dutiful school children who never steal a glance
                                              out the windows
at fur-and-bone dogs chasing dogs of wind.

Day-a-page calendars give
each twenty-four hours its chance in the light.
August 2nd is more itself
without the 1st or 3rd touching its elbows.
In old movies, dates proud on their islands
turned over so fast they went watery —
now a quaint trick, laughable — but would
a fast-forward digital race of red numbers
catch the passing of weeks so well? Would we
miss the silent *flick-flick-flick* of days, paper

floating, disappearing beyond the frame?

2

On his fiftieth birthday, he recalls so clearly
the humiliations of being twenty
that for a few moments the years since
are swallowed up in smoke:

he stamps his feet again on a street corner
after midnight, globes of snow collecting
in his eyes, melted by his tears,
while at last he sees he will be alone

forever, bundled and cold-eared, his body
filled with longing like a tree
with sap; then, a quarter-century on,
he recalls the morning after his son's birth

when he bought a white rattan rocking chair,
carried it over his head a mile uphill,
placed it by the woodstove and tried it out
for the first time, empty-armed,

though now that his son has reached eight
the day he carried the rocking chair uphill
is no more or less clear
than the night of tears and snow.

3

Is time a moth, a vulture, a paper plane? Are we
    talking of an owl's slow soundless descent
or the crude creaking of some da Vinci contraption
    made of sticks, leather, and wheels?
To a girl behind a locked door having her first taste
    of a boy's lips (or the inside of her arm?)
time is a hummingbird restless and aglow
    sipping every flower in the wallpaper,
while her grandfather a floor below — a new
    widower, his old dog with its nose in his palm —
watches the play of darknesses outside the window,
    time crisscrossing the yard on its pterodactyl wings.

Time Stands Up for Itself

you are the dark line, the crack
forking through all the broken pottery
that ever was unearthed.
Why, you don't even have the interest
of a villain; there's no dark complexity
to you — you're dull.
                    — Brent MacLaine, "A Lecture to Time"

O cousin of the chimpanzee, don't fool yourself:
like any creature, you're a thing of time.
Your poor metaphors try to trap me
but you can't save or spend me. I'm vaster
than any coinage ever minted; you can't
slip me into a wallet of Italian leather.
Whoever cooked up the phrase "the march of time"
deserves an F: no swinging arms and brass band
contain me, no spectators snap pictures of me
with the kids, or limit me to wheels turning
through flyers, fruit peels, and horse dung.

I am the space between heartbeat
and heartbeat.
              Without me the pottery I crack
would never have been moulded.
I make possible the seed's swelling,
the root's delving, the infinitesimally slow grinding
of sand from stone.
                   Gargantuan and grim, yes,
but I've got laughter up my sleeve
at your watches given torture tests,
the Christmas someone unwrapped six calendars

from six friends, Crusoe digging a notch
into a stick each morning. Without me,
bats in caves couldn't judge the milliseconds
between echoes; there would be no caves,
no *while, before, after, ago.*

Yes, I am merciless,
but I'm mercy too: the pea-sized egg
of the bee hummingbird, the cantaloupe-sized egg
of the ostrich, stay warm in my cradle.

Pause for a moment,
imagine my disappearance — world submerged
in frozen ink, unimaginable zero —
then call, call me back from the edge —

The Floral Clock

James Neil, *Rays from the Realms of Nature;*
or, Parables of Plant Life
(London: Cassell, Petter, Galpin, & Co., 1880)

Linnaeus appears to have been the first
to form a blooming dial. On the living face
each hour was marked by the opening
or closing of petals. As the habits of many plants

are not quite regular, we have been at some points
to select the most accurate time-keepers.
Every minute of the day may be marked
by one of 120,000 species.

Yellow Goatsbeard, called by country folk
Joseph's Flower, awakes at three o'clock.
The brilliant azure Wild Succory, or Chicory,
of chalky cornfields, uncloses at four.

The pale Common Nipple-wort opens
at five, Buttercup about six. At seven
White Water-lily rears it chalice to the light.
Scarlet Pimpernel and rarer Proliverous Pink

both open at eight. The golden star
of the Lesser Celandine, such a lover of the sun
it will only unfold its petals on bright days,
gleams forth at nine . . .

... Nottingham Catchfly
bears a flower which looks withered
and shriveled during the day
but spreads out its glistening white petals,

full of fragrance, at six in the afternoon.
Evening Primrose, released
from the curiously hooked ends of its calyx
at seven. Night-blowing flowers like these

attract those insects bearing
the pollen of one blossom
to the pistil of another. How could such hours
be reckoned but with herbs and flowers?

Brier Island, Spring Weekend

Wizened, blackened,
    last year's rosehips
wind-shaken, still attached

                            Bone-coloured, wind-buffed
                            dead trees lift limbs —
                            ghosts incarnate in wood

This driftwood has the face
    of an extinct, unnamed
flying reptile

                            Spruces slanted one way:
                                sea winds humble
                            all verticals

His baby in a sling
   at his chest, that father turns
a beetle right-side up

By a rippling pond
   a perched kingfisher, more still
than its own reflection

After so many hopes
   answered, at dusk
we hope for owls

Nasal mating calls —
   woodcocks in the dark
field by the graveyard

A word for the air
  in the gaps between
a vulture's wing-tip feathers

4 bobolinks, 8 goldfinches
  jotted down — but I find
more than the sum

One toad's long clear trill
  cuts through spring peepers'
tintinnabulation

After I touch the bark,
  my word for the day
becomes "bioluminescence"

Gulls, ranked among rocks,
　　shriek, look every whichway:
Parliament is sitting

　　　　　　　　　　Speckled rock in gull's nest —
　　　　　　　　　　　at a glance, hard to tell
　　　　　　　　　　from the pair of eggs

The cluster of nesting straw
　　in that gull's beak
is bigger than its head

　　　　　　　　　　The sea's hand, the sea's breath
　　　　　　　　　　　bestow rust
　　　　　　　　　　on driven spikes, a pile of bolts

Sheet of tin on shore,
   now all rust, fragile
as an old manuscript page

                              Gaudy orange rubber glove
                                 pokes two fingers
                              out of heaped kelp

What carrion beetle
   will bury this car tire
washed high ashore?

                              Today's Grand Prize goes
                                 to the disemboweled fridge
                              inspected by sandpipers

Without family
    for a few days, I watch
young and old seals lounging

                                    Magnifying glass:
                                        give us the barnacle's mouth
                                    gathering air, like ours

Four blues — that jay,
    that sky, that sea,
that roof through bare alders

                        Fell asleep
                            reading a novel of the world's end —
                        woke to the sleepless waves

Whites of Pennant Point

But for conifers' cold greens, whites
      hold this day in their thrall — sky shaded
ivory, curdled-milk ice spanning
      puddles, boulders like flecked-salt mounds,
flutterings of snow lifting lightly and
      settled. These are shadings
into which have crept the faintest
      pinks and yellows; blink, the subtleties
change. Titanium White, Zinc
      White, Antique Silver, Honied White,
Divine White, Hush White. Surely
      this is a planet to be born on
keeping such beauty past
      so much diminishment.
From the left, a soundless arrival,
      stainless wings folding: a Great Egret
sinks its feet in shallow snow:
      another white, the most alive yet,
the other side of ravens deepening
      the darknesses of moonless nights.
All these whites wash your vision
      like a watercolour from the early
Ch'ing Dynasty — then
      from the bird's throat a croak
breaks. Could *that* be the voice
      of a bird like an apparition,
that sound rough as rocks clashing,
      earthy with humour, a belch

from the back row? What were your ears
    hoping for, a flute like spring water?
Your lungs capture the contradiction
    on this face-numbing edge of the North Atlantic.

Pearly Everlasting and Others

Namelessness
hovers over all, infuses all.
Like lines webbing a fractured lens
the names in our eyes clutter our views.

In other minutes, we feel increased lightness,
a slight shrinking of distance, when we say
Meadowsweet, Evening Primrose, Morning Glory.
Bringing our fingers to the tiny points tipping
six petals, we say Blue-eyed Grass.
After placing our faces close
to Viper's Bugloss and Deadly Nightshade
a sense of counterbalance sets us aright
with Sundew, Steeplebush, Solomon's Seal.

A ballpoint keeps track
in the pages of a pocket-sized blank book.
Listing, you say, a kind of love. The namers
are long-gone, anonymous, this their bequest.

Along the loose bank, Pearly Everlasting lifts
cottony stems into the light. On the beach
we bend to taste bits of glaucous leaves,
to know in our bodies why
Mertensia maritima is *Oysterleaf.*
You imagine a planet on which everything
has the middle name Forget-me-Not.
I call out for you to cross the rocks as far
as the low, crawling, alien Heal-All.

Notes

Epigraphs: The Ammons poem appears in his collection *Diversifications* (Norton, 1975). The passage from the script of Wenders' *Wings of Desire* was written by Peter Handke.

"An Offer of Warmth": Quotations from Heraclitus are by Brooks Haxton from *Fragments: The Collected Wisdom of Heraclitus* (Viking, 2001).

Part 3, "Given Words": The epigraph for this section comes from "The Wisdom of Falling," an interview with Don Domanski by S.D. Johnson in *Where the Words Come From: Canadian Poets in Conversation*, ed. Tim Bowling (Nightwood, 2002).

In this section of found poems, all words and sentences are taken from sources named under the poem titles. In many cases I've shortened the chosen sentences, but I've made it a rule to add no words. The art of writing these poems is one of radical selection, concentration, and free rearrangement. In many cases, a few sentences were picked from hundreds of pages. The closest precedent may be Annie Dillard's *Mornings Like This*, which provides a valuable preface about this sort of found poem. Sue MacLeod's "How-To Poems" were also an inspiration. Many of these poems favour books and other documents I inherited or received as gifts.

"My Father's Birth": When Lester Bradford Bartlett was born on November 17, 1925, in the Chipman Memorial Hospital in St. Stephen, New Brunswick, his father may have been reading the day's edition of the provincial newspaper, *The Telegraph-Journal*. A gift for my father, this poem was created 81 years later. In section 3, "The raccoon" is a substitute for the original's "Bobby Coon," one of the characters in Thornton W. Burgess's animal stories for children, which ran in a daily syndicated newspaper column throughout North America, uninterrupted from 1912 to 1960.

"A Short History of Shelters": I inherited the book by March from my maternal grandmother Clara (Camick) Wills.

Luther Lawrence, with
one of his granddaughters,
ca. 1895

Luther Lawrence's
phrenology plaster head

"Head Sketches": O'Leary's phrenology book belonged to my great-great-grandfather Luther Lawrence (1815-1903) and was passed down to me, along with the phrenologist's plaster head Luther used for his hobby.

"London, in the Beginning": The two books used for this poem were bought second-hand by my grandmother Clara Wills in 1937, and given to me about thirty years later.

"The Breeze Made Such Music": I found Prothero's book in a used-book sale in 1974. The poem was written in honour of my uncle Hubert Bartlett (1929-2005), who read, recited, and taught the Psalms to thousands of parishioners and visitors, friends and strangers, over several decades, in many communities.

"What He Chose to Record": My great-grandfather C.B. Lawrence of Bayside, New Brunswick, was a descendant of several generations of New England and New Brunswick ancestors; the husband of a first-generation Canadian with Irish parents, Minnie MacFarlane, who died of liver cancer in 1905; the father of five daughters and two sons; president of a local Agricultural Society from 1910 to 1935, and, for shorter periods of time, County Councillor and Warden.

"Early Readings, 1908": I inherited a copy of this reader from my grand-mother Georgie Othelia (Lawrence) Bartlett. I've imagined her at lunch on the grass in the shadow of her one-room schoolhouse, browsing through the book. The authors quoted are Anon., Charles Dudley Warner, Anna Sewell, Thomas Carlyle, Anon., Hans Christian Andersen, Alfred Lord Tennyson, Francis Parkman, Mark Twain, and Charles Dickens.

"Dear Georgie": When he wrote the letters quoted here, my great-uncle Hermon Lawrence was twenty years old, and his sister Georgie was twenty-two. The Dwight mentioned in the poem was their brother.

Clara Wills, 1925

"My Mother's Birth": On December 15, 1928, Marjorie Lou Wills was born in Lancaster, New Brunswick. Decades later I often saw my grandfather closely reading newspapers, folding their pages in half for easier handling. I imagine him reading these excerpts with divided attention, awaiting the birth of his second child.

"First Lessons in Symbiosis": Six years after the publication of *Strange Partners*, which was published when hopes for the United Nations were still high, I found a copy of it at a used-book sale.

"Fragments from 2073": Thirty-five years before the writing of this poem, the book by Harding was given to me by my great-aunt Pauline (Camick) Hooper of Eastport, Maine.

*

"on teaching Purdy's 'The Wine-maker's Beat-Étude'": My lines *I talk/ like a dog, laugh like a man, bark like God!* are a corruption of Purdy's *I bark like a man / laugh like a dog / and talk like God.*

"One Minute on a Planet": This poem owes a debt to John Burroughs' essay "In Mammoth Cave," in *Riverby* (Houghton Mifflin, 1894), and to "The Island of Auks," a chapter in Franklin Russell's *The Secret Islands* (Norton, 1965).

"The Floral Clock": At a second-hand sale in 1967, I bought a copy of Neil's book for 25¢. Two four-leaf clovers pressed in it may be over a century old.

Acknowledgements

For their sprightly conversation and crucial suggestions while this book was being written, from 2001 to 2007, many thanks to workshop friends — especially Rose Adams, Johnny Barger, Dee Dwyer, Tonja Gunvaldsen Klaassen, Jill MacLean, and Sue MacLeod. I also deeply appreciate the generous, unstinting attention Anne Compton gave to these poems. I could hardly hope for a wiser, more dedicated editor.

Much gratitude to everyone at Goose Lane, for the gifts of their energy and perfectionism. To my father, Lester Bartlett, for gathering the ancestral photos and giving me C.B. Lawrence's diaries. And to the editors of the following journals and anthologies for first publishing these poems, often in earlier drafts:

Arc: "Travels of the Watch"

Body Language: A Head-to-Toe Anthology, ed. John B. Lee (Windsor: Black Moss, 2003): "For Anyone with a Body"

CBC Radio: "Ghosts of Pier 21" (This poem was a response to a commission from producer and poet Barbara Carey to write a poem set in a favourite "local site." The CBC production of the poem was recorded on site at Pier 21 in Halifax.)

CV2: "Ghosts of Pier 21"

The Antigonish Review: "Early Readings, 1908," "What He Chose to Record"

The Fiddlehead: "One Minute on a Planet," "Time Stands Up for Itself," "Saint Mary's U Études: *on teaching with a cold; on teaching Poe's 'The Fall of the House of Usher' the 12th time; on teaching Dickinson's poem 260*"

The Gloriatur (Kentville: Gaspereau Press, 2007): "One Minute on a Planet"

The Goose (on-line): "First Lessons in Symbiosis," "Floral Clock"

Lichen: "Head Sketches" (as "Brutal Sketch"), "Fragments from 2073," "A Short History of Shelters"

The Malahat Review: "All the Train Trips," "Dear Georgie," "An Offer of Warmth," "Thumbnail Biographies"

Maisonneuve: "Poems Among the Ads"

The New Quarterly: "Saint Mary's U Études: *on teaching* The Tempest; *transcendental graffiti; on listening to a first-year student read Bishop's 'One Art'*"

Nthposition.com (on-line): "Grieving Mountain," "The Verdict" (as "Imprisonment"), "Spiders Magnified"

The Parliamentary Poet Laureate website: "The Sideways 8"

Queen's Quarterly: "Three Candles and a Fan," "Walking Laura Home from Daycare"

Rampike: "6364 Edinburgh St."

Saranac Review: "The Breeze Made Such Music," "Playground, May Day," "Saint Mary's U Études: *on teaching Purdy's 'Wine-maker's Beat-Étude'; on skating after teaching Avison's 'Butterfly Bones; or Sonnet Against Sonnets'*"

Twenty-five Years of Tree, ed. James Moran and Jennifer Mulligan (Buschekbooks: Ottawa, 2005): "All the Train Trips," "Time Stands Up for Itself," "Travels of the Watch"

Several of the poems also created the limited-edition chapbook *Travels of the Watch* (Kentville: Gaspereau, 2004)